Copyright

The Sidekick:
Adult Coloring Book

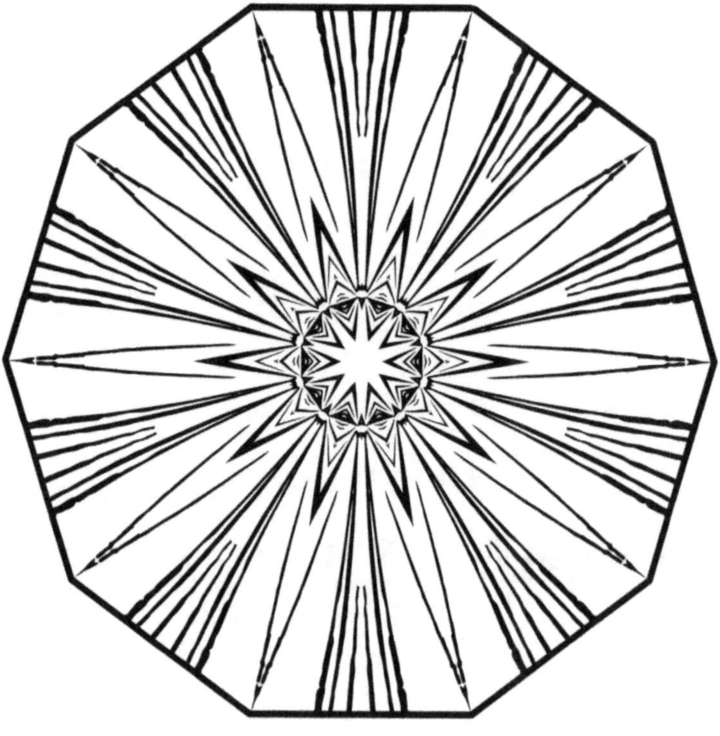

Howard Hinton Jr

Reminders Plus Photography LLC

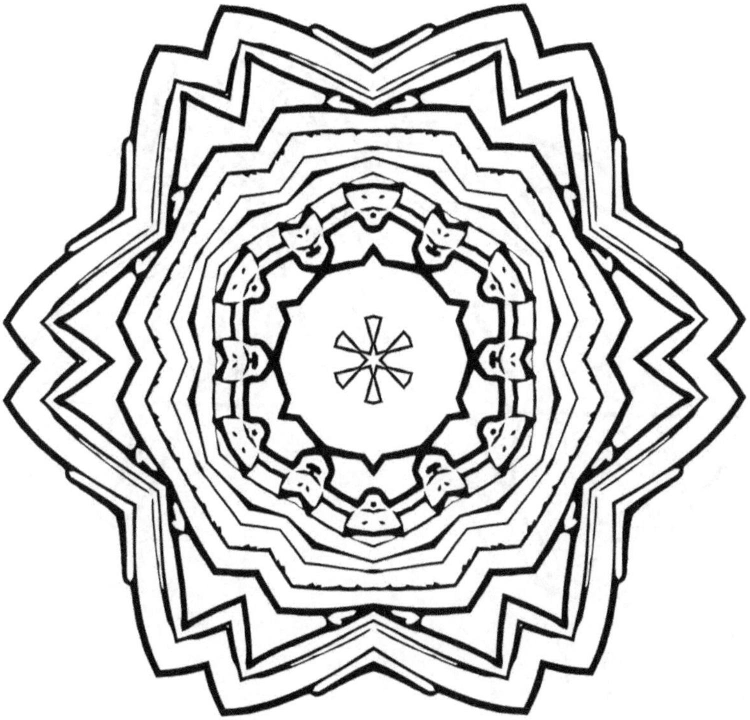

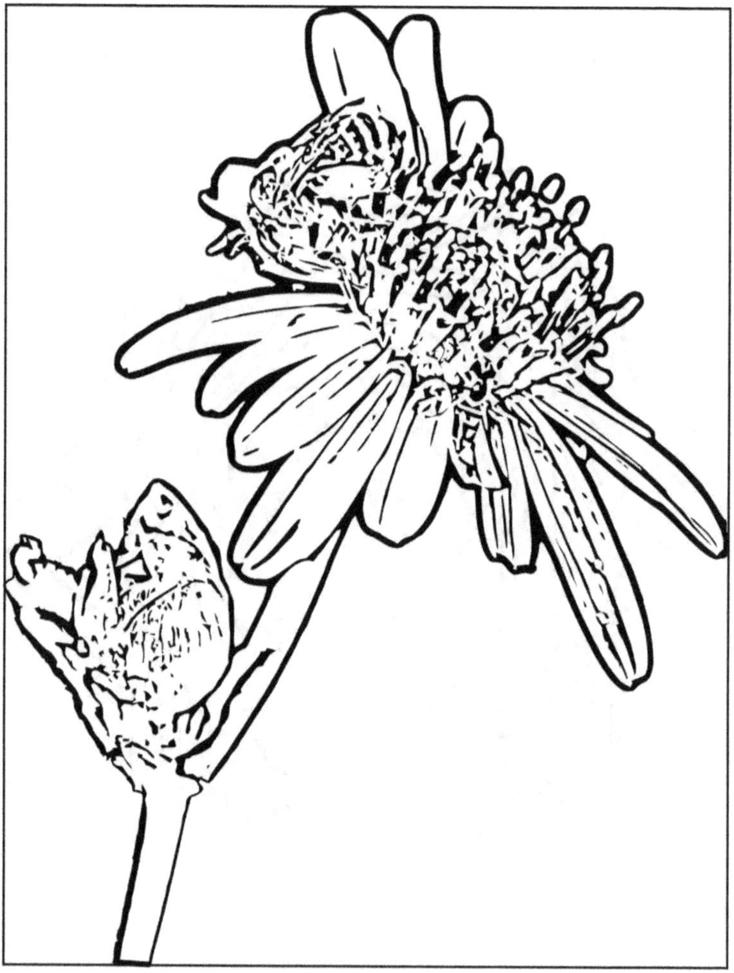

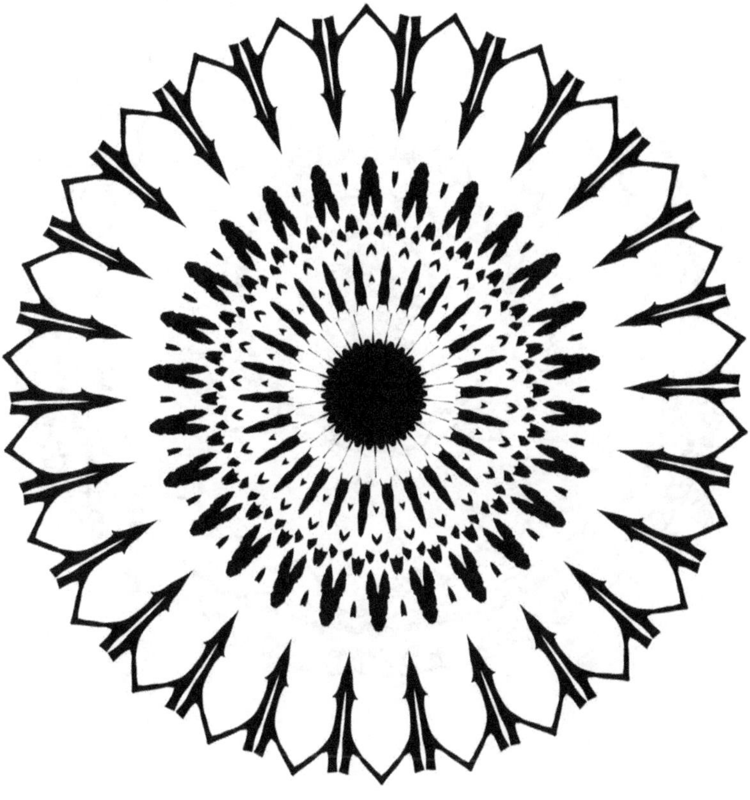

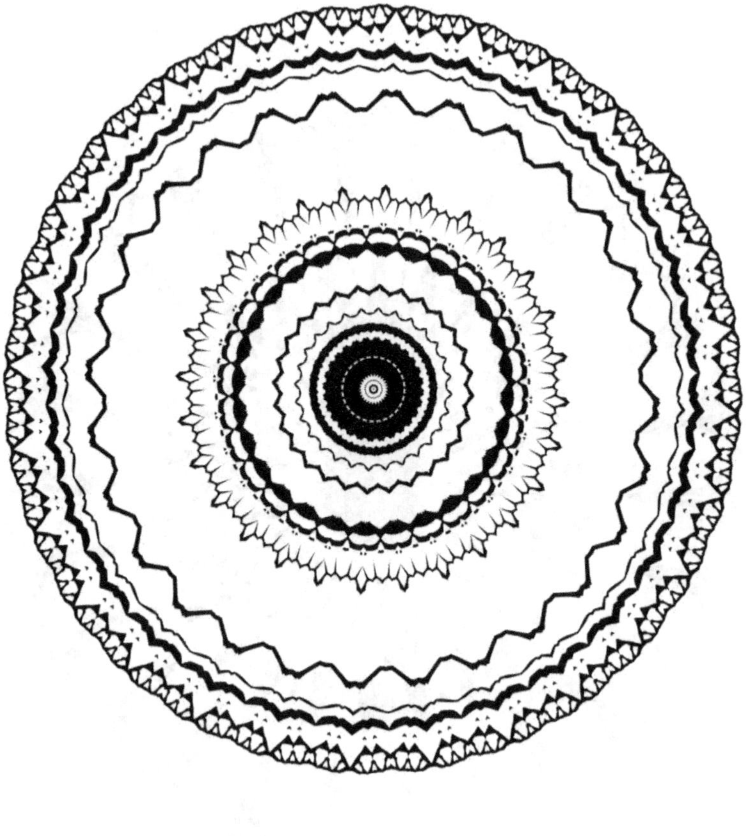

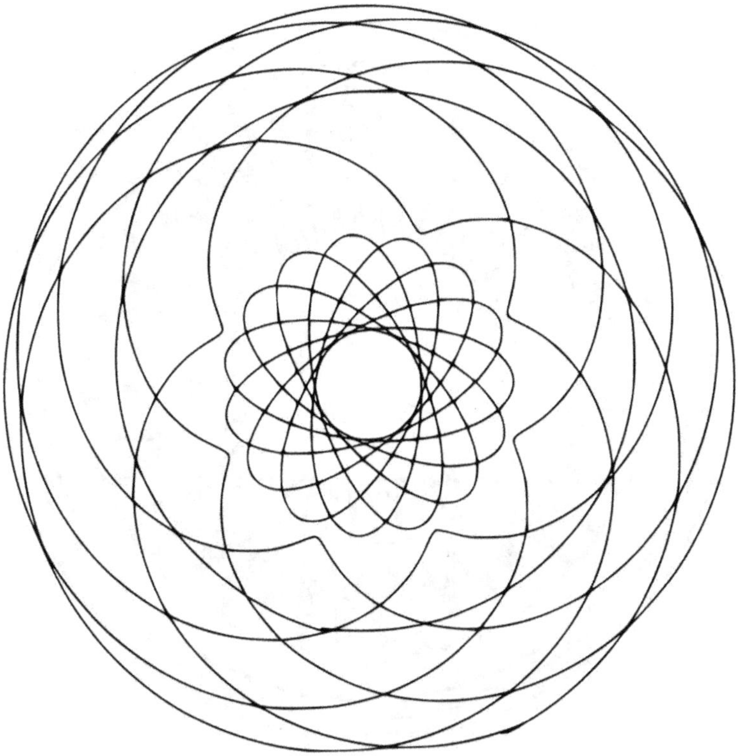

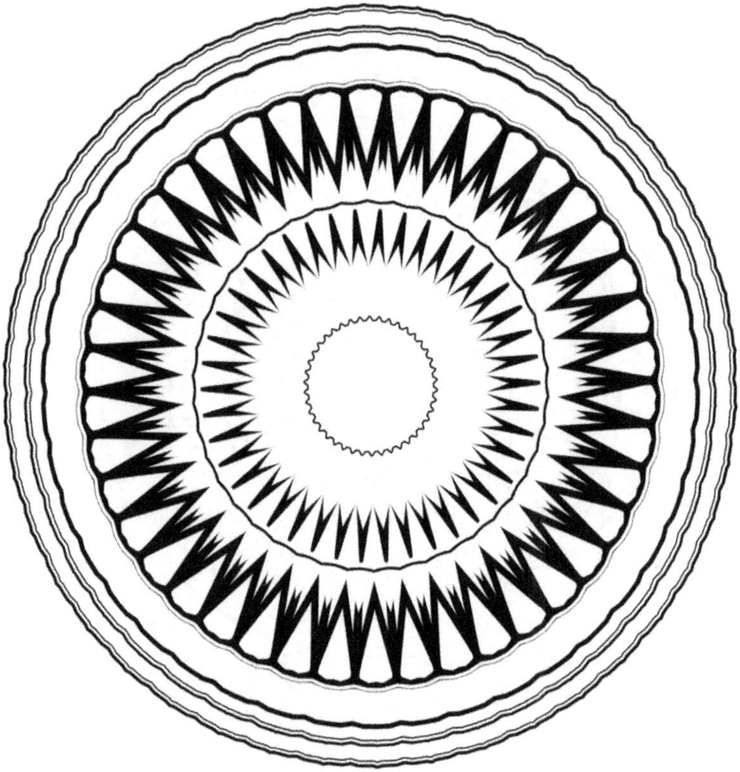

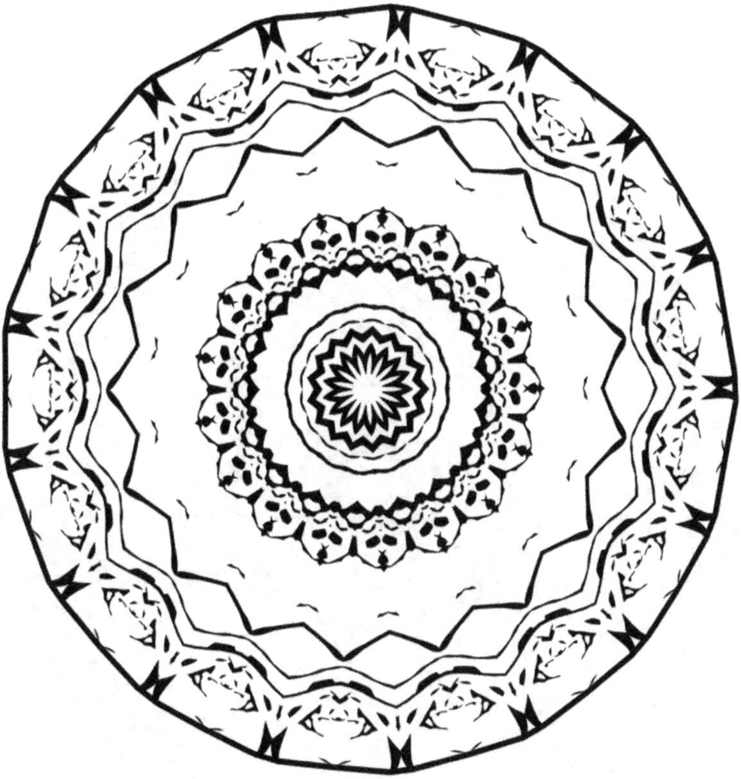

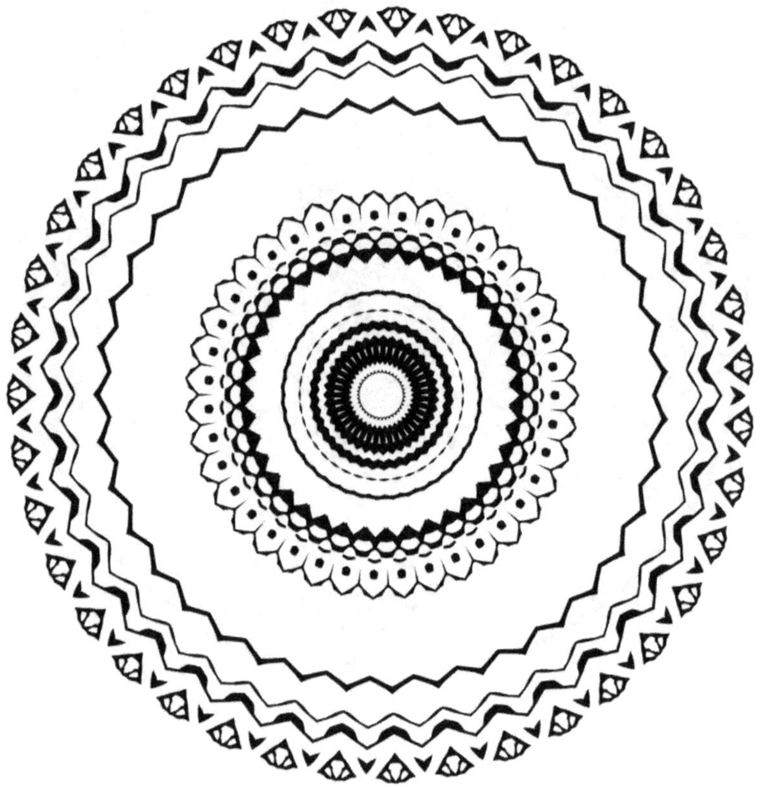

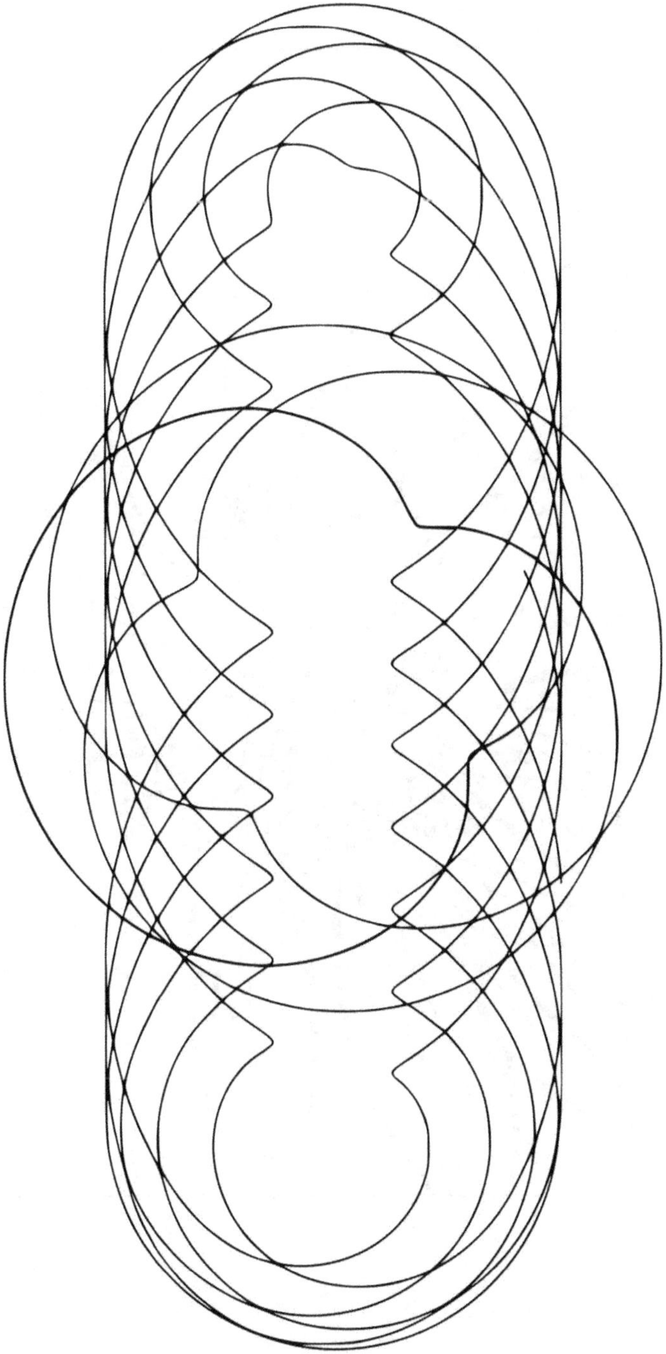

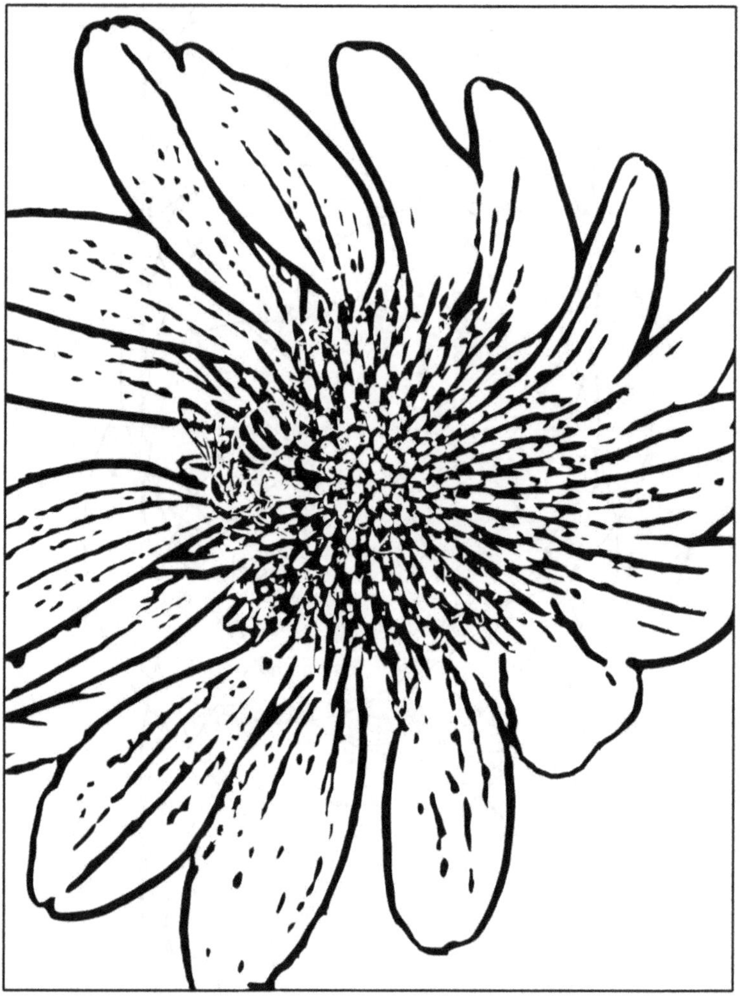

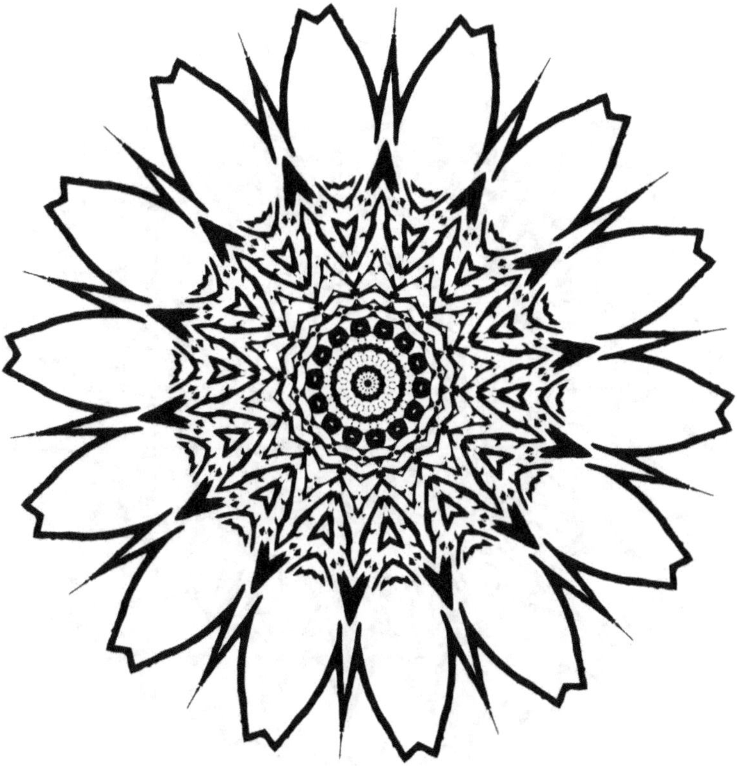

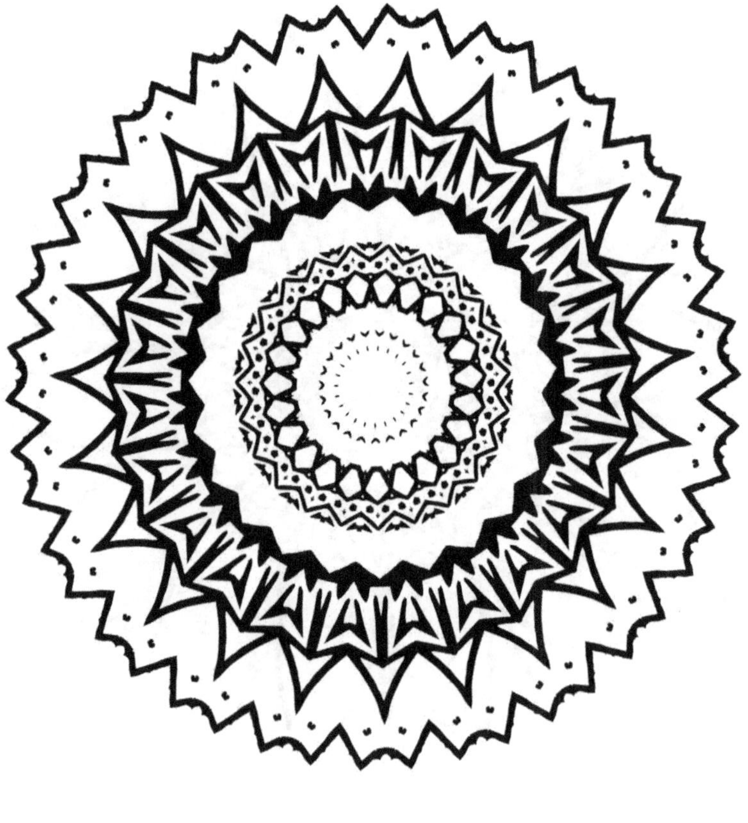

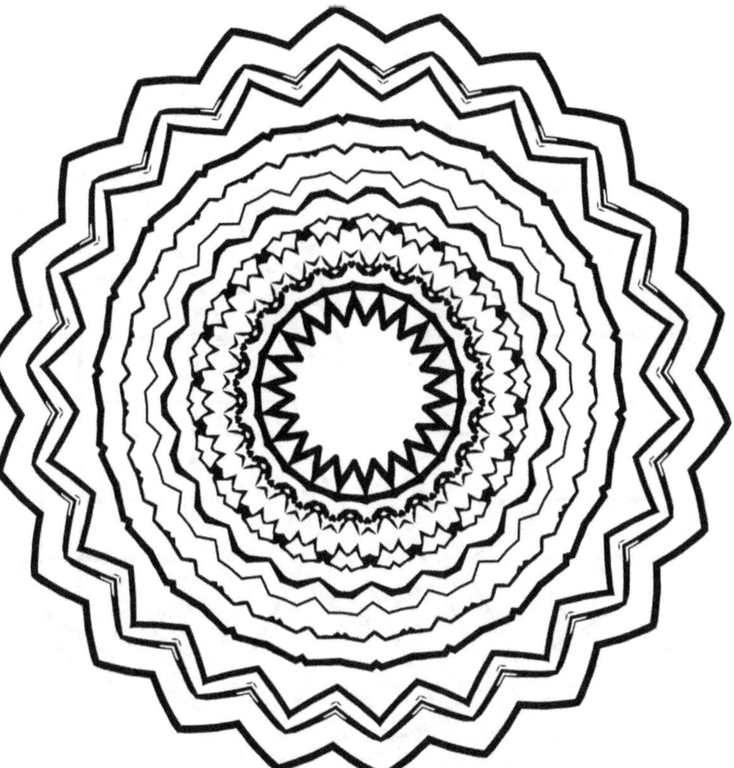

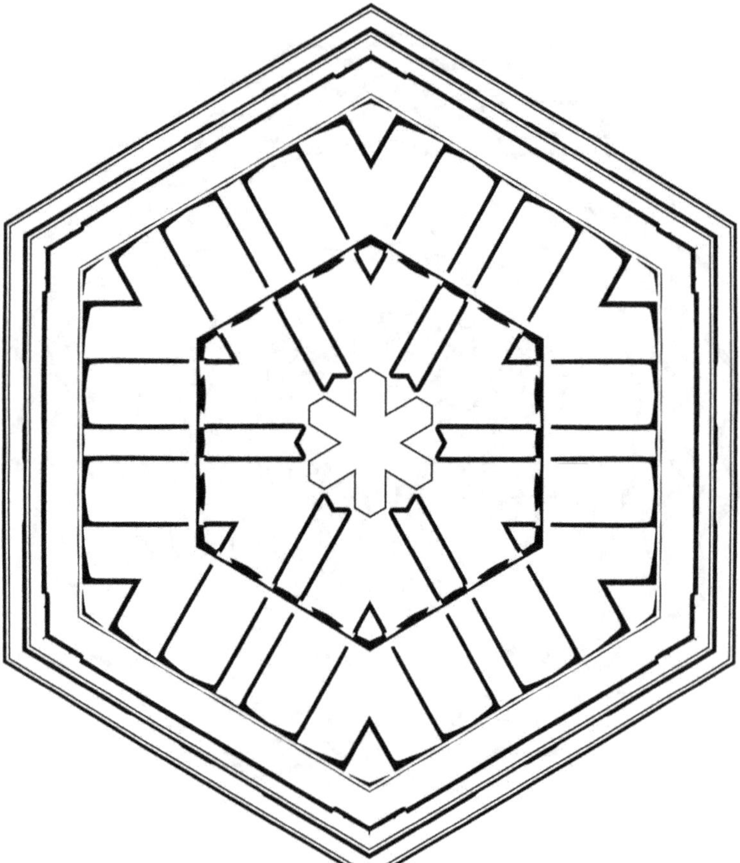

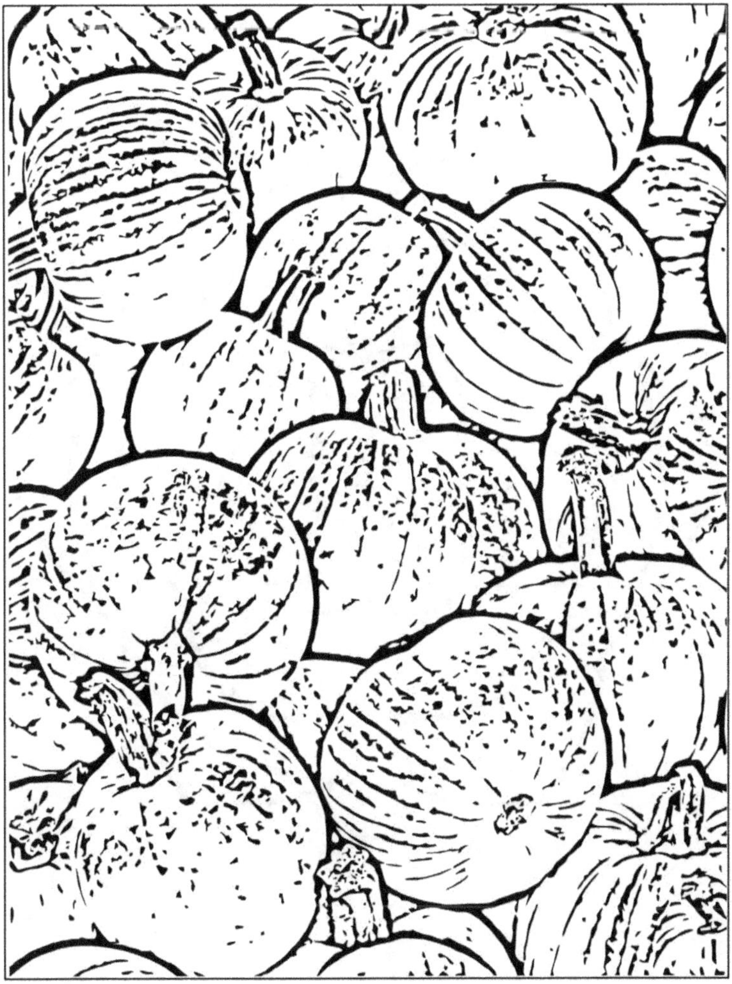

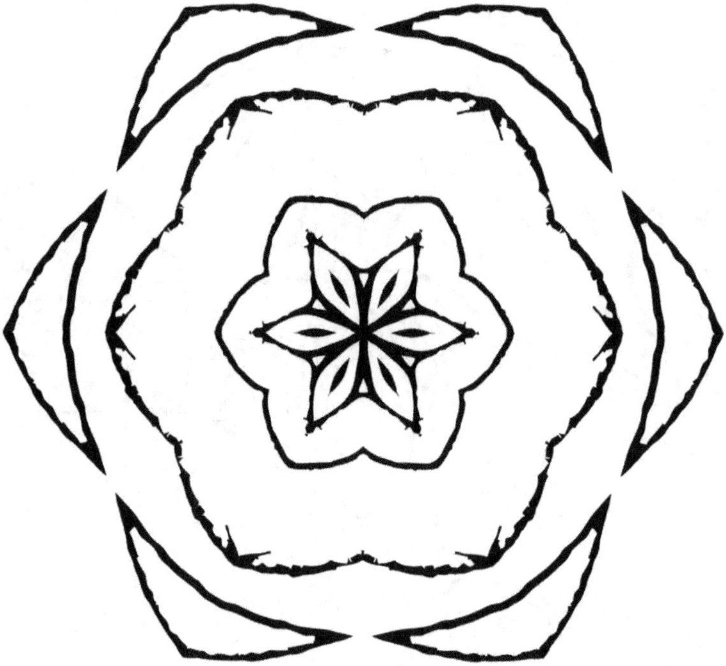

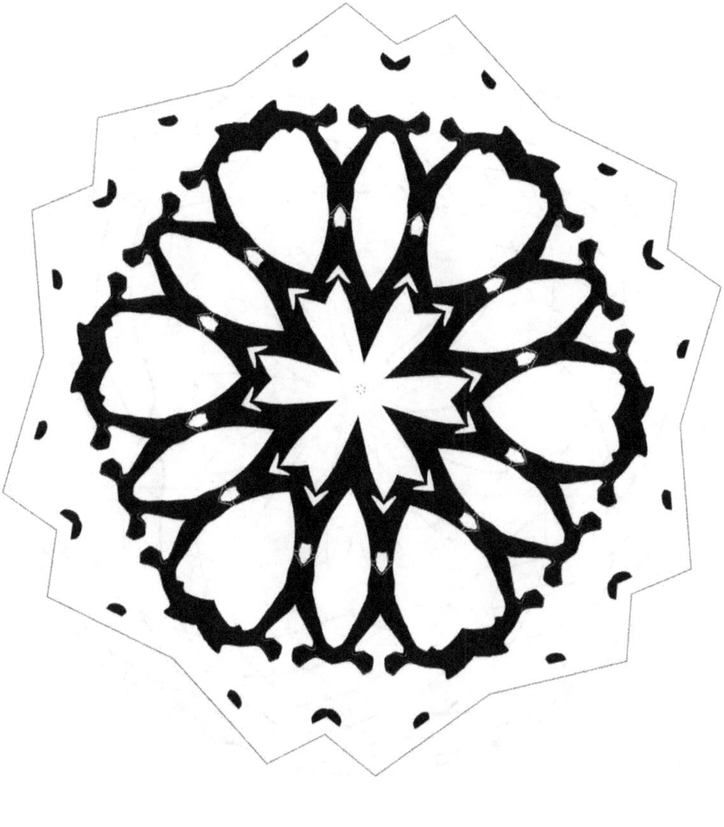

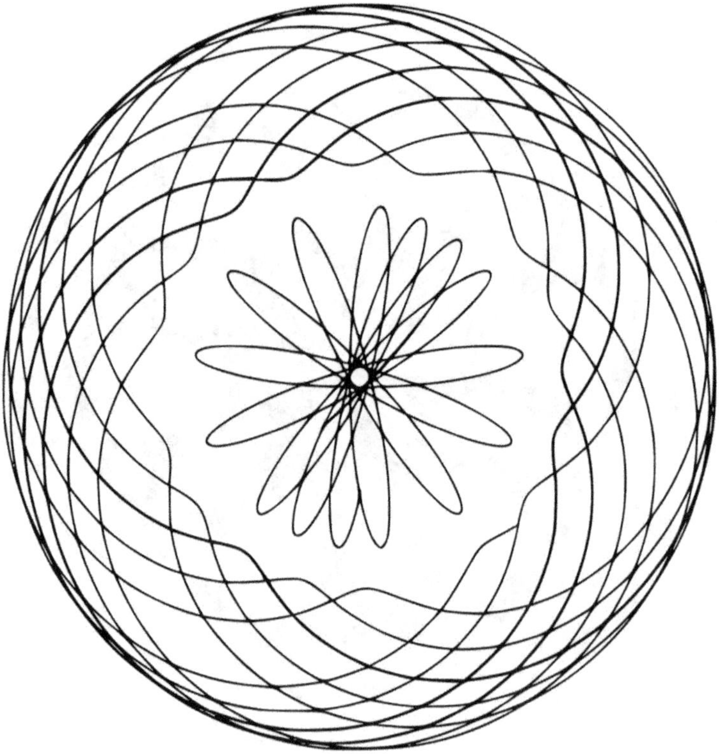

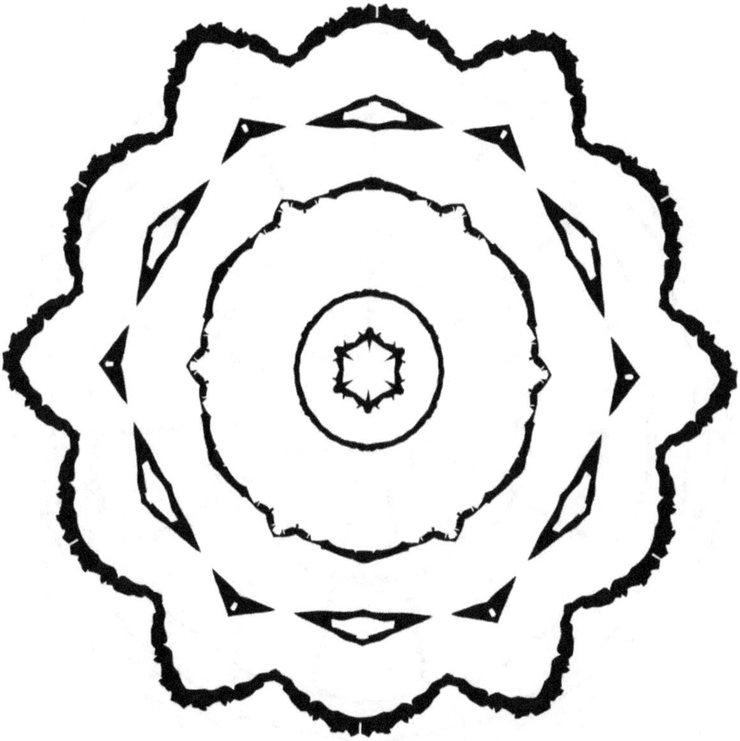

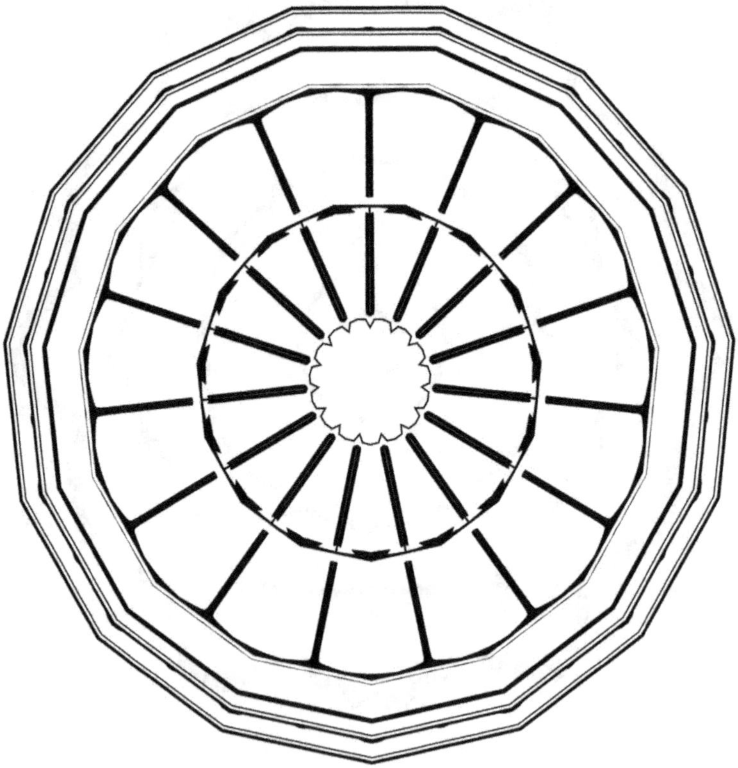

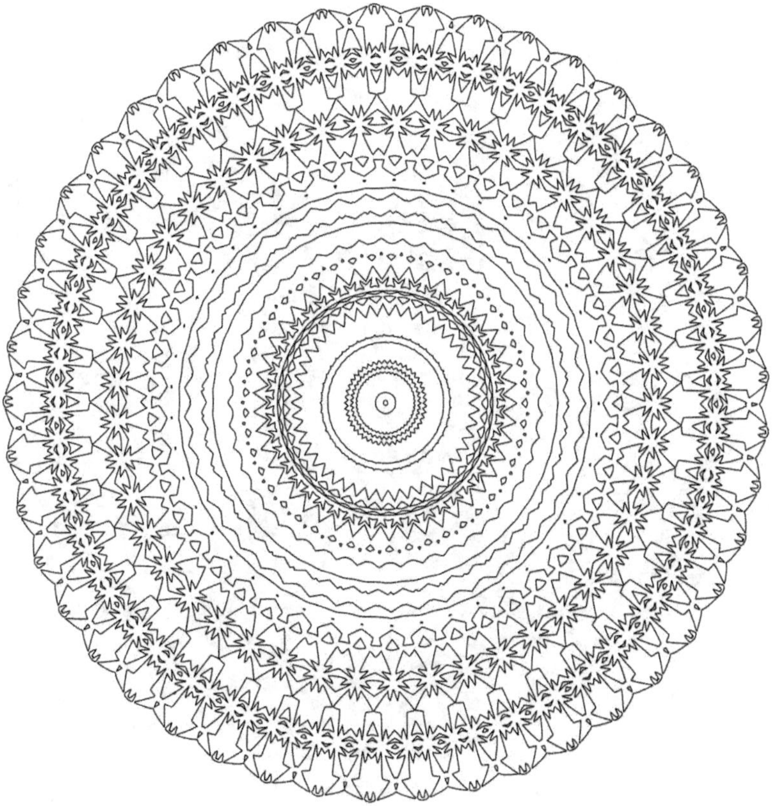

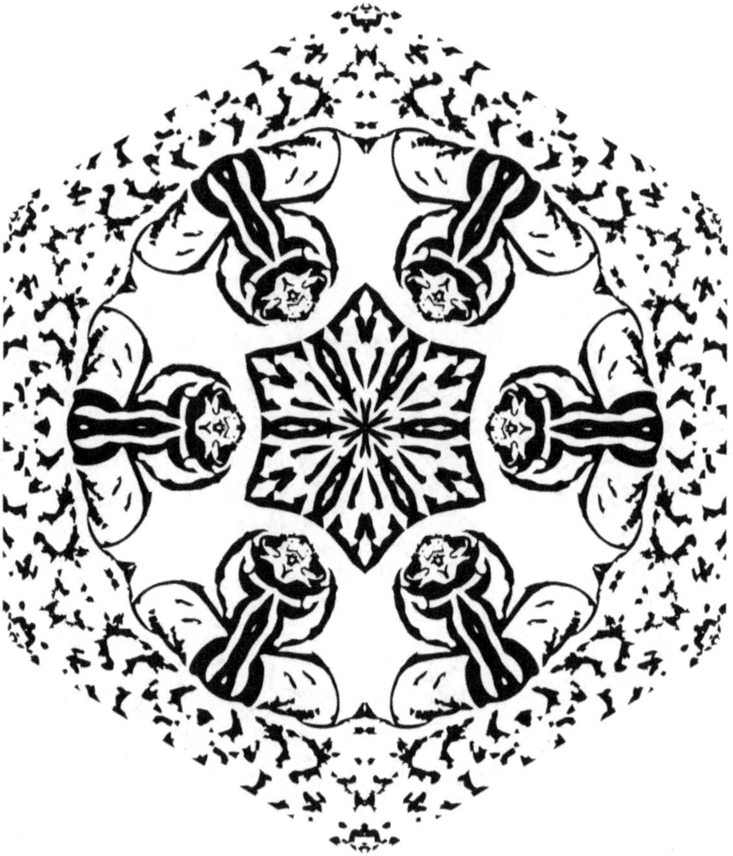

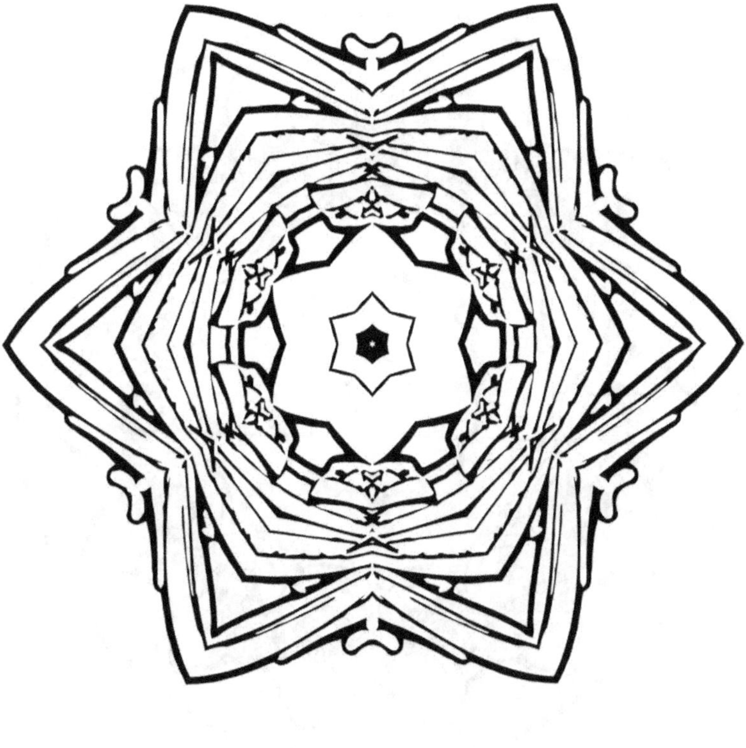

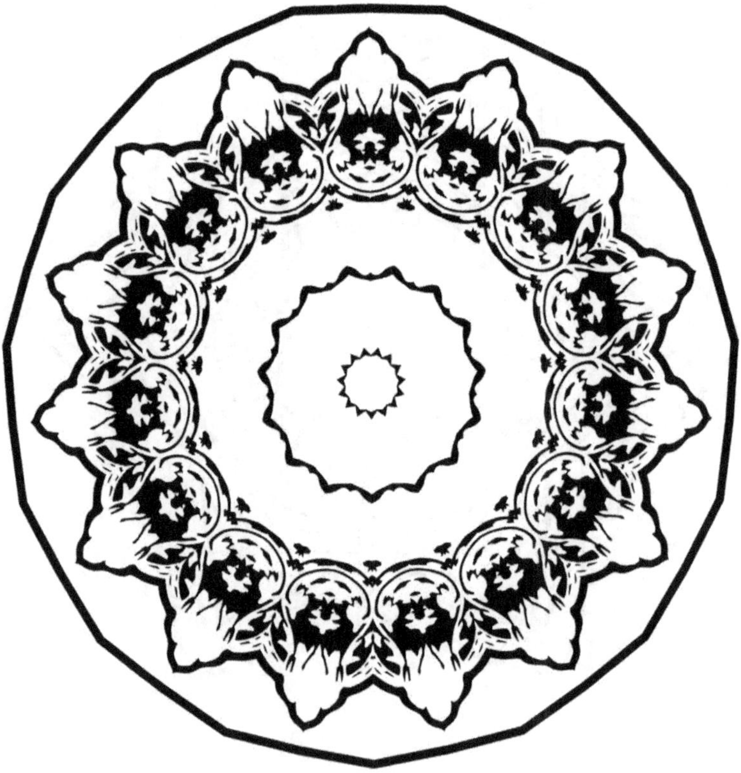

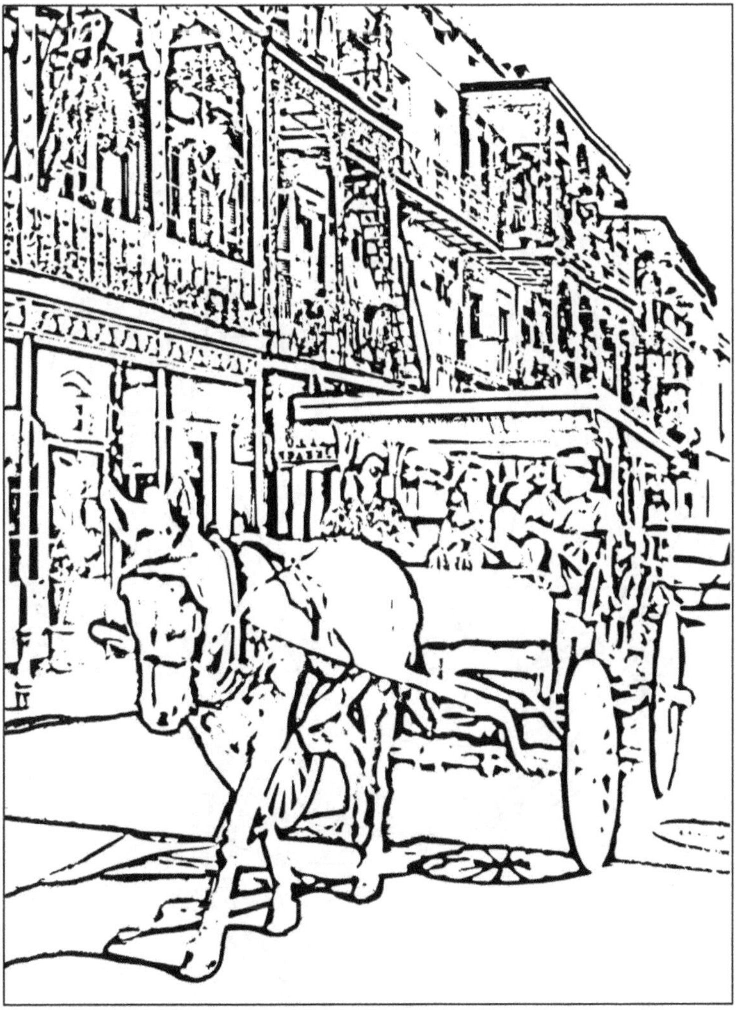

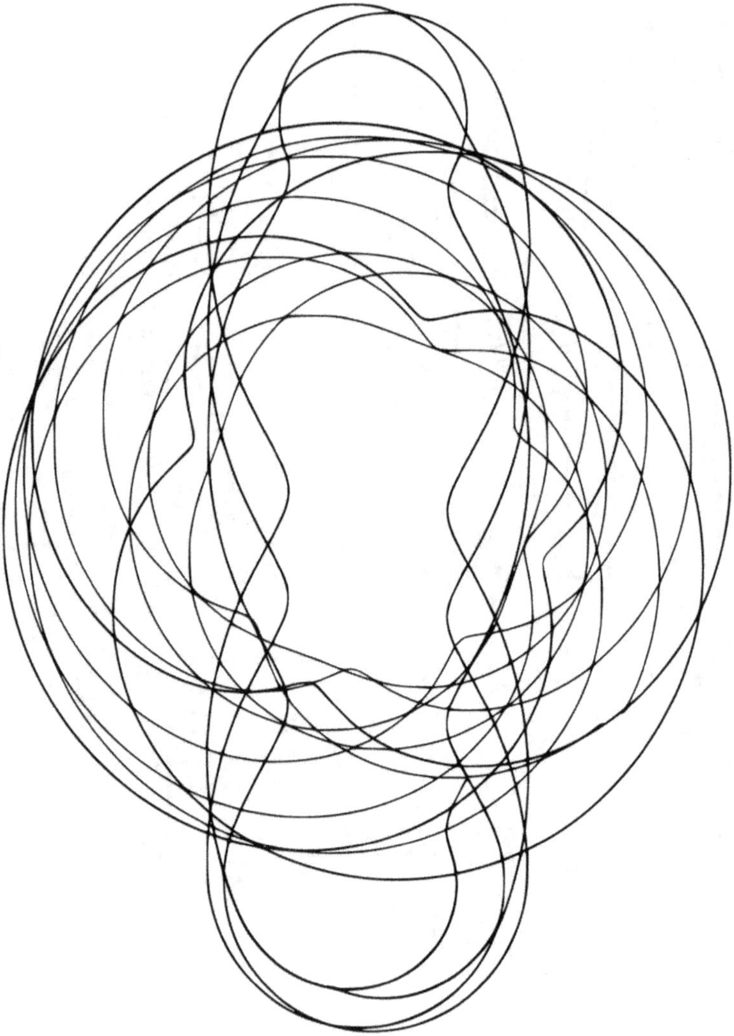

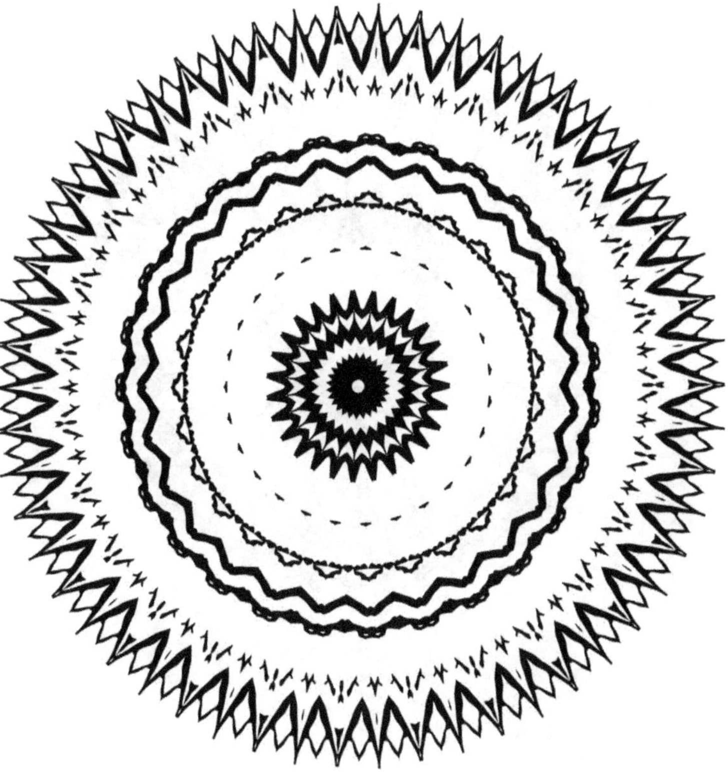

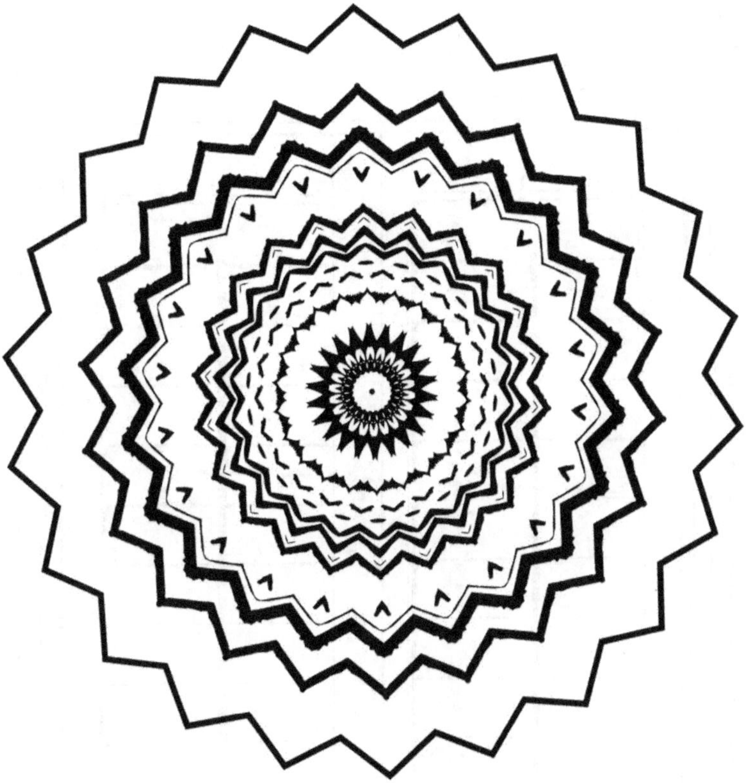

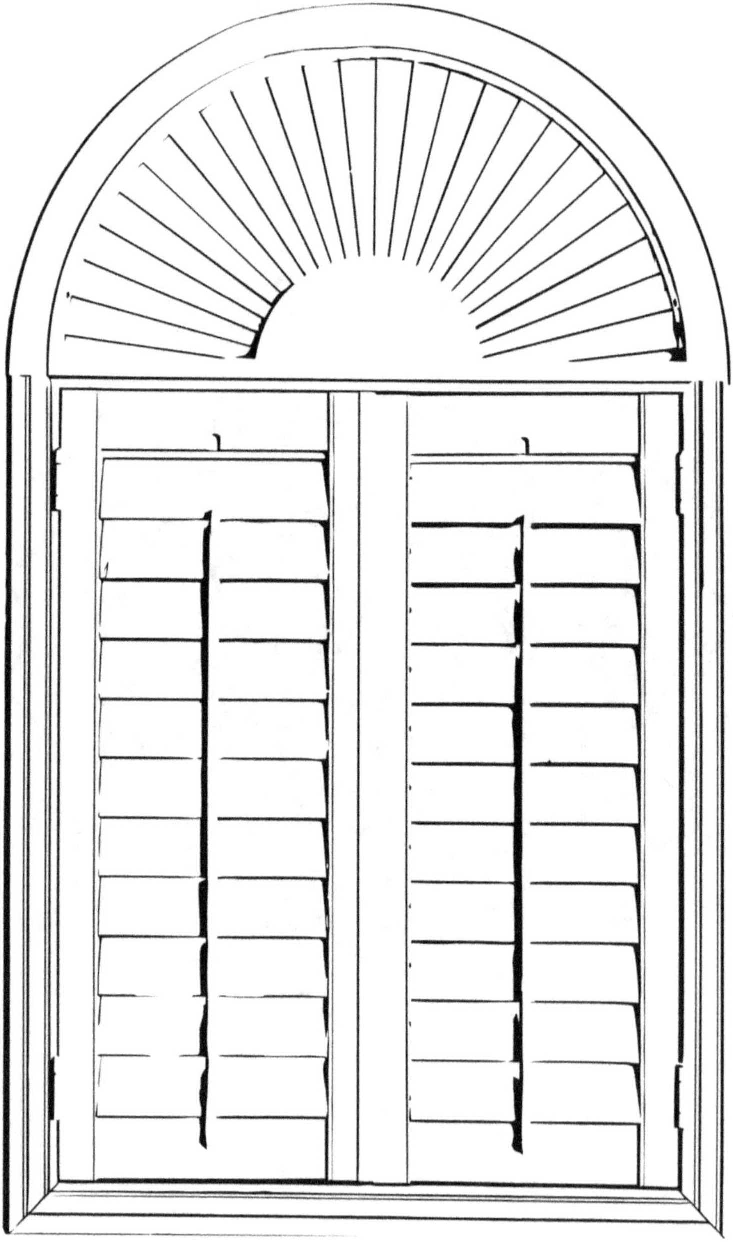

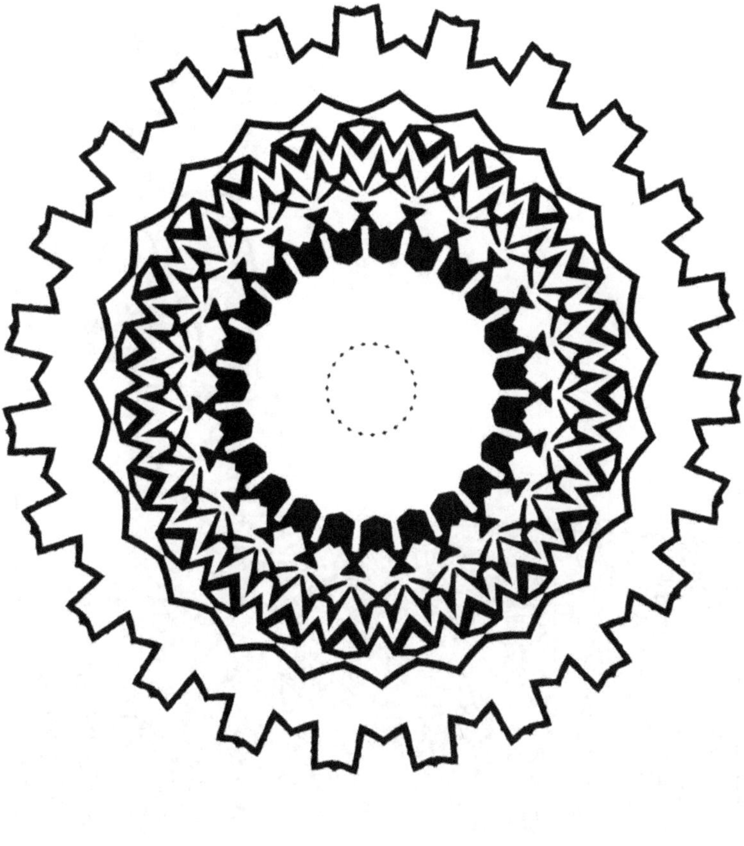

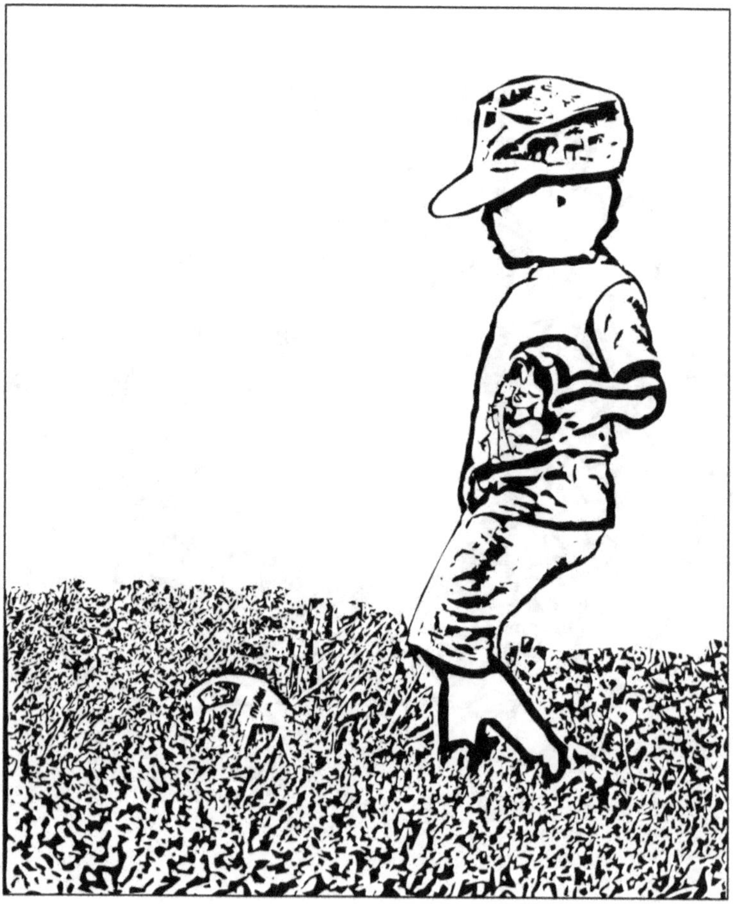

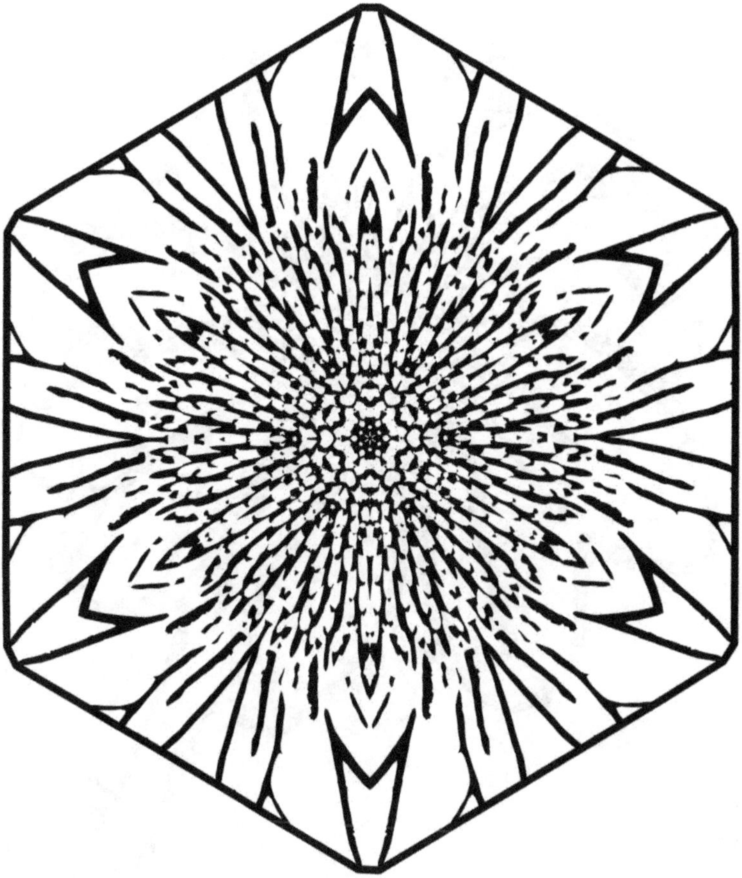

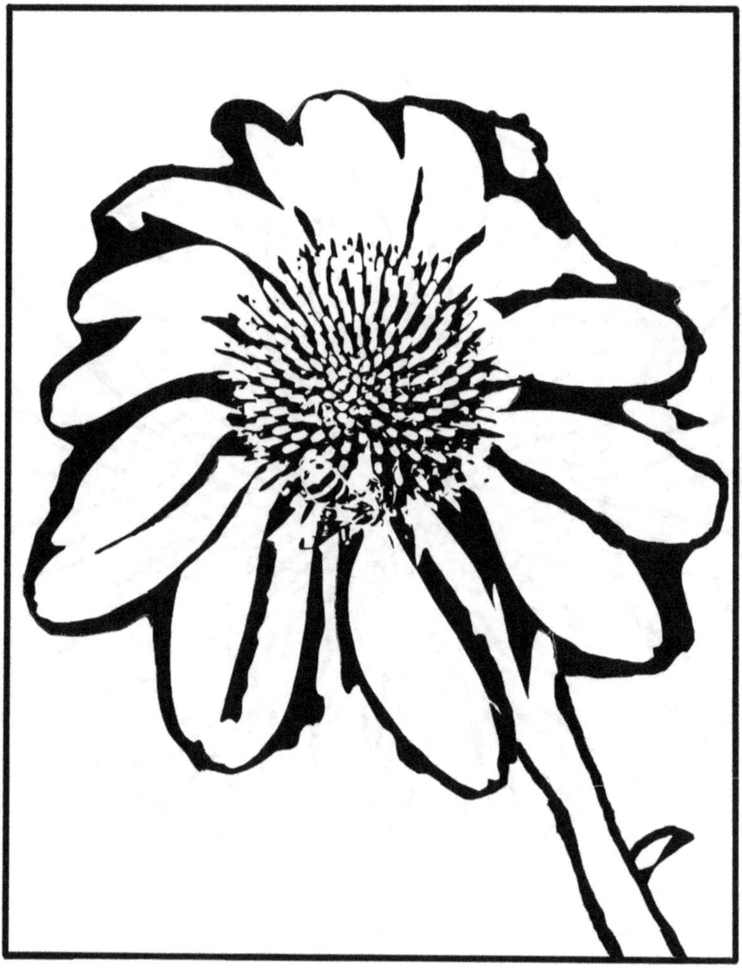

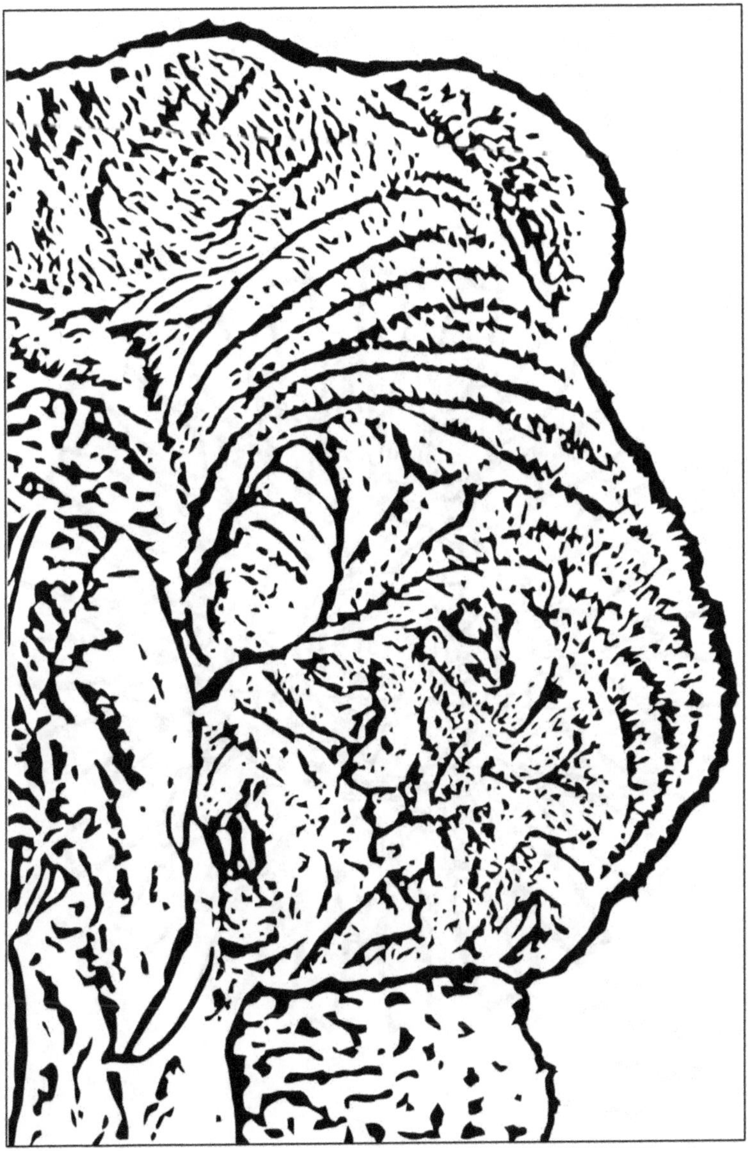

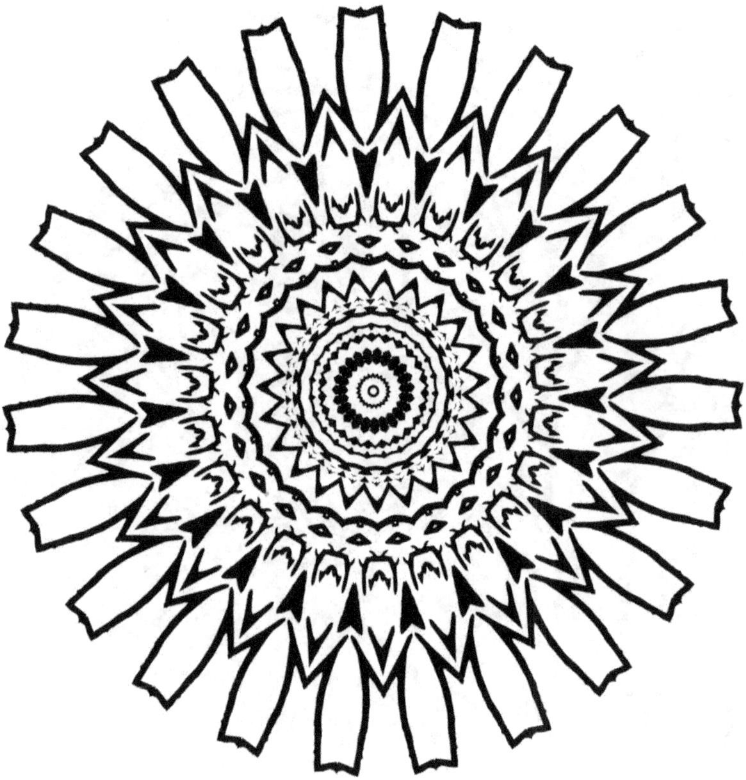

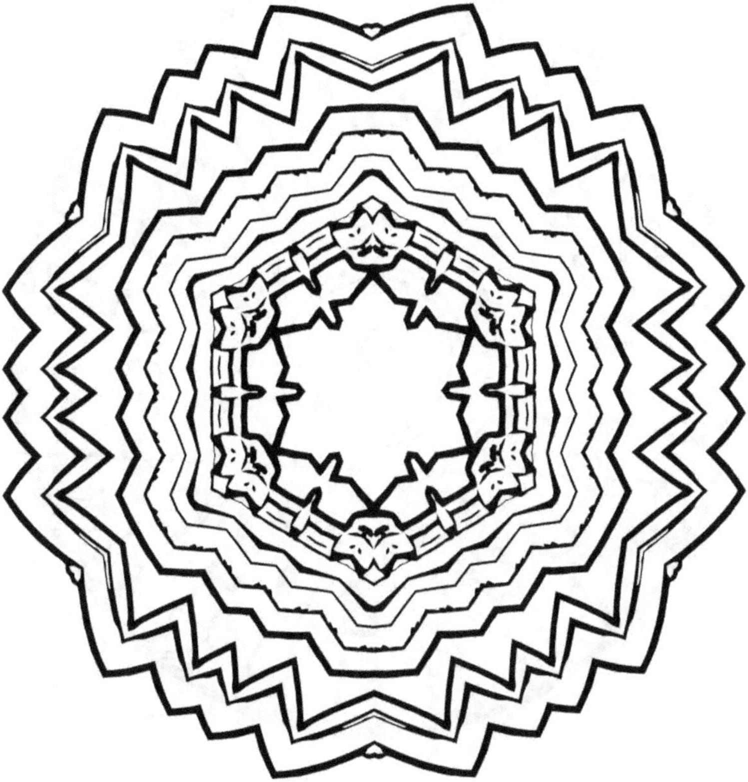

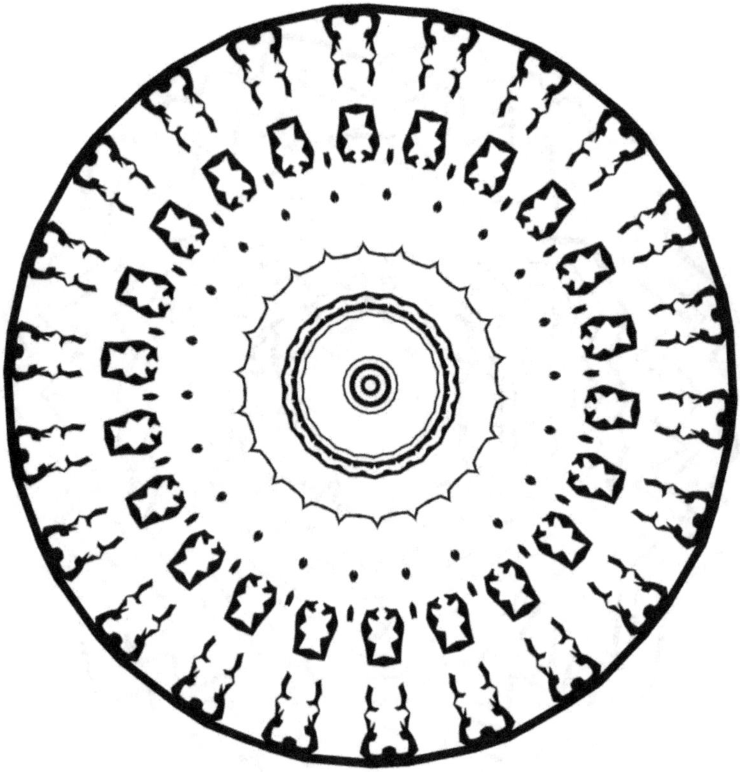

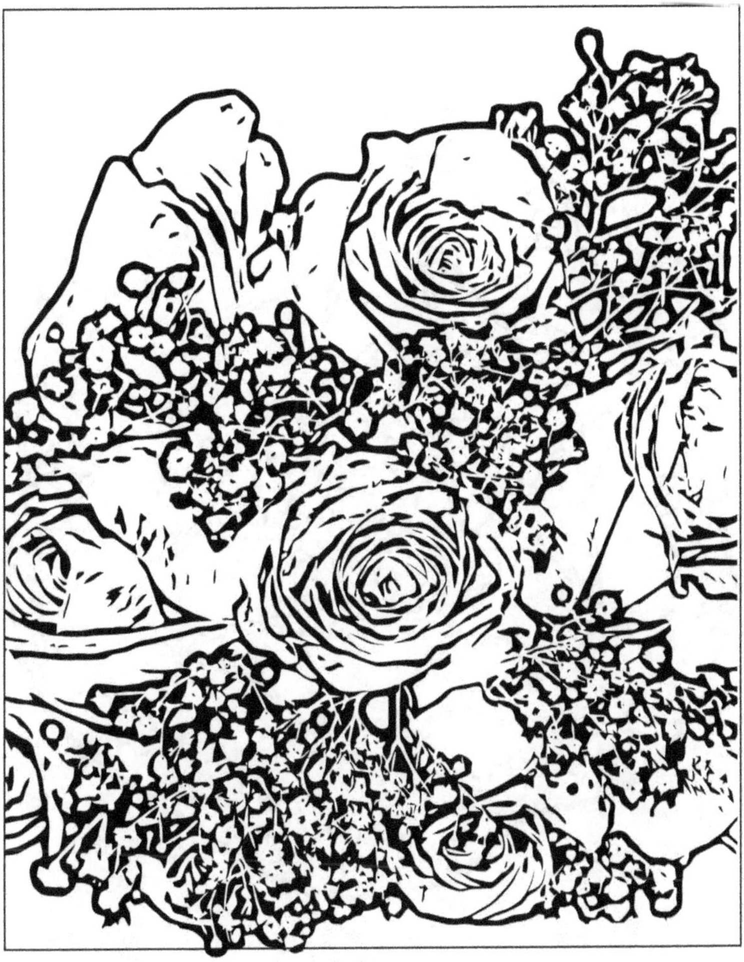

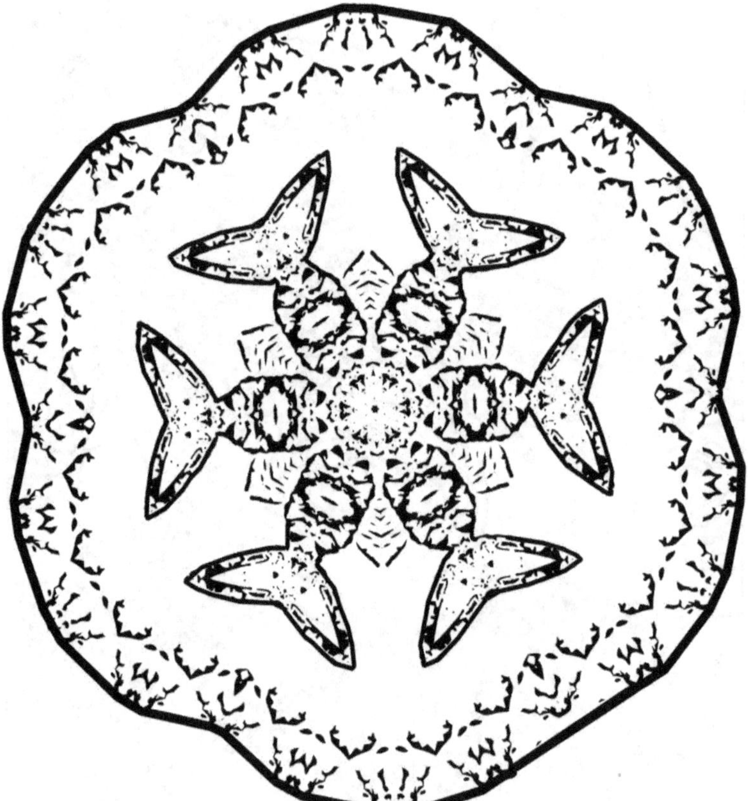

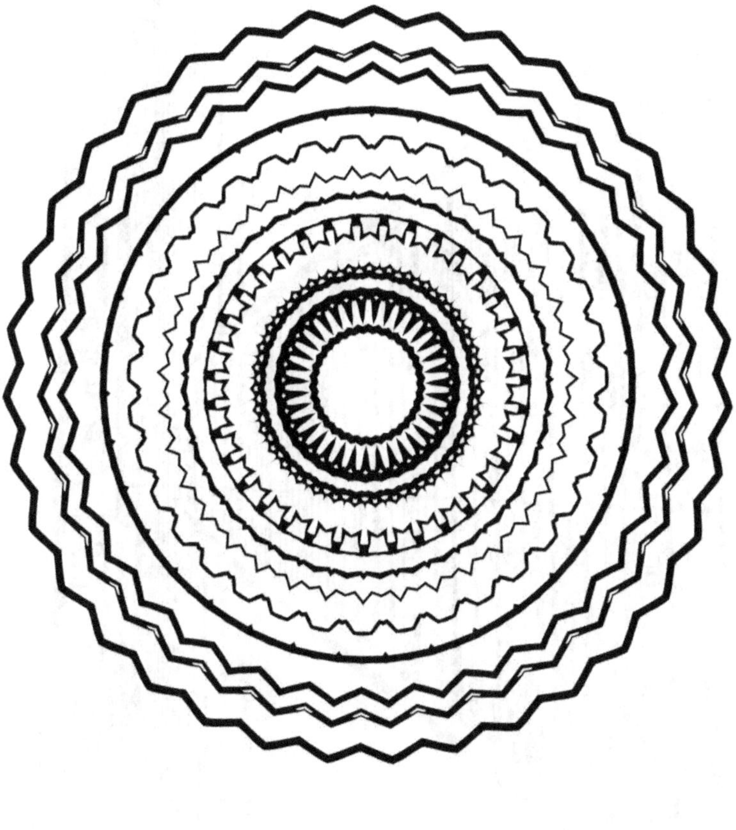

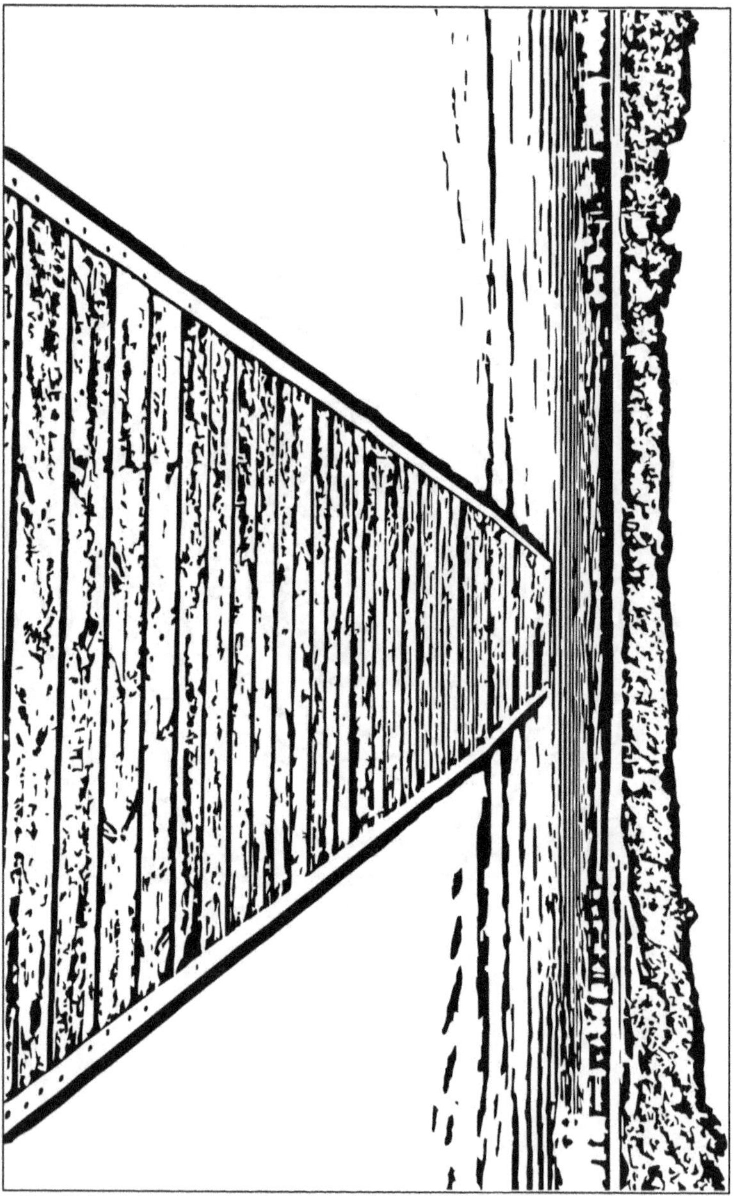

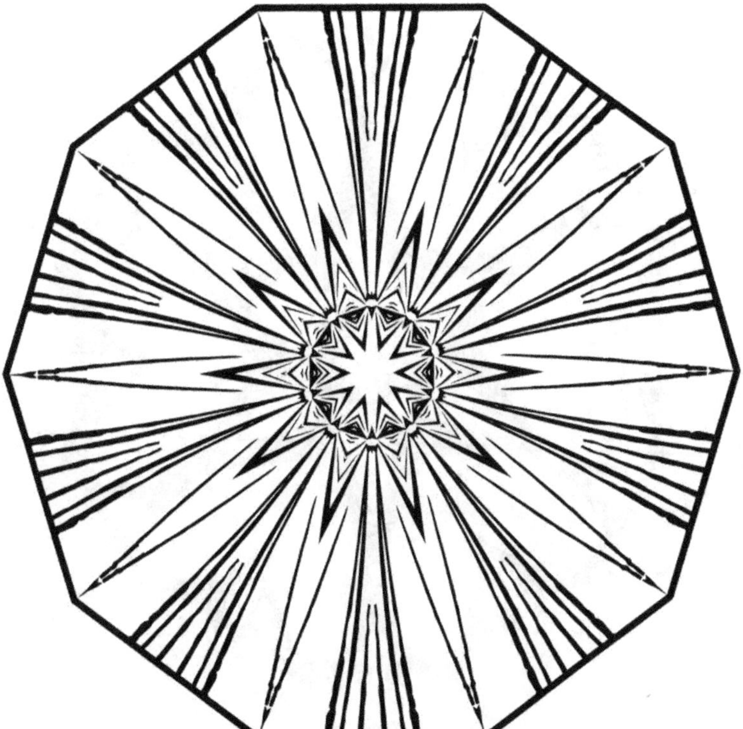

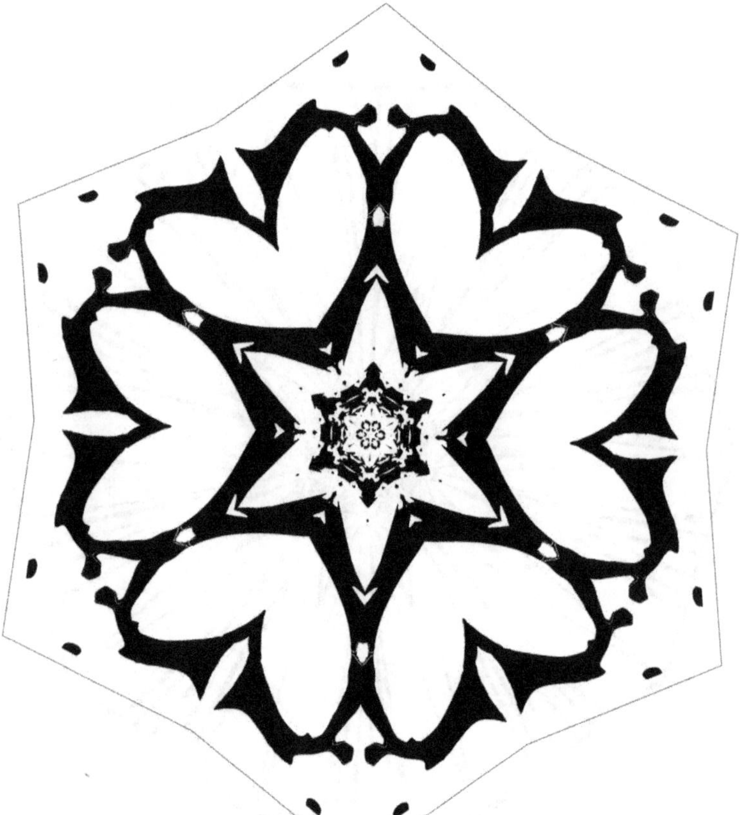

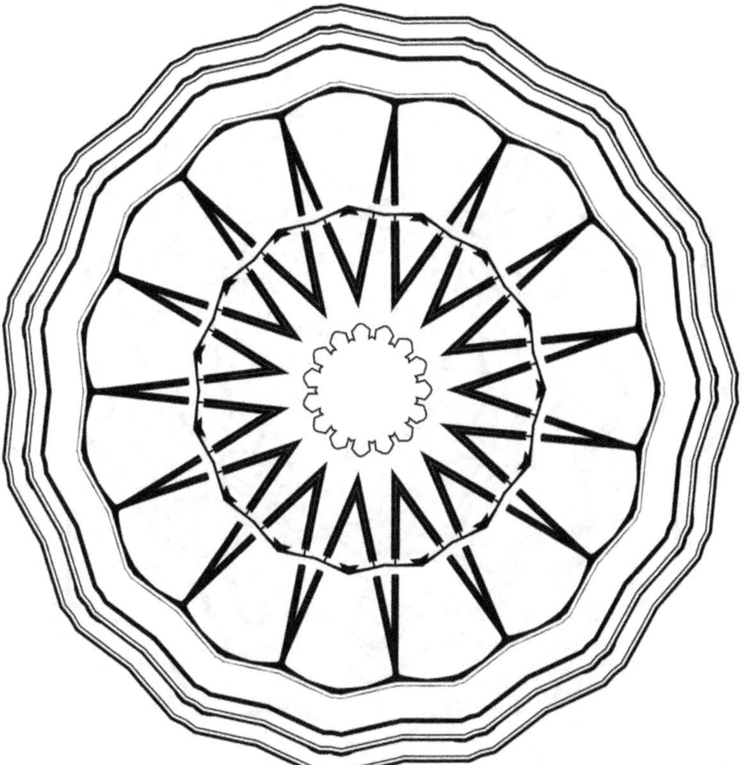

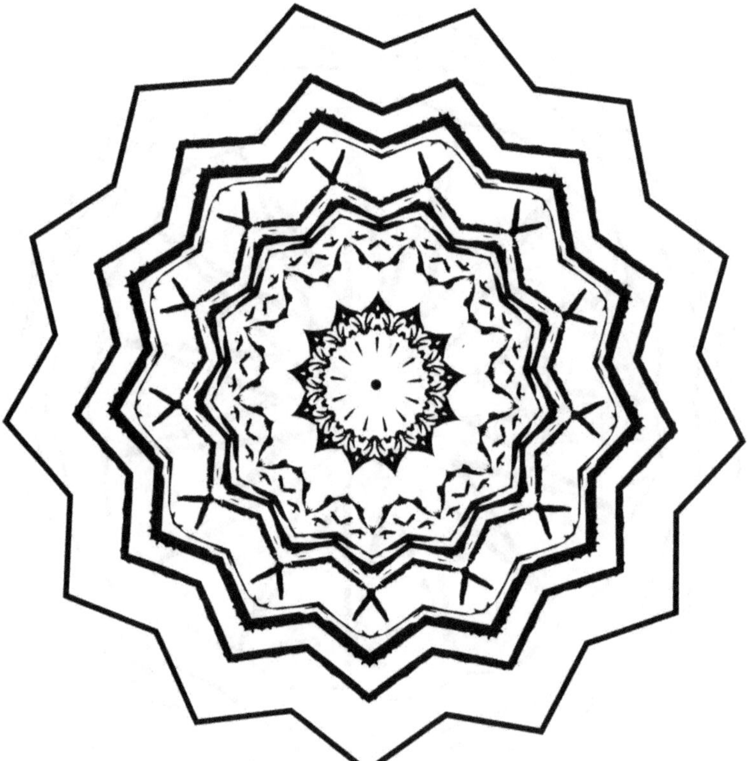

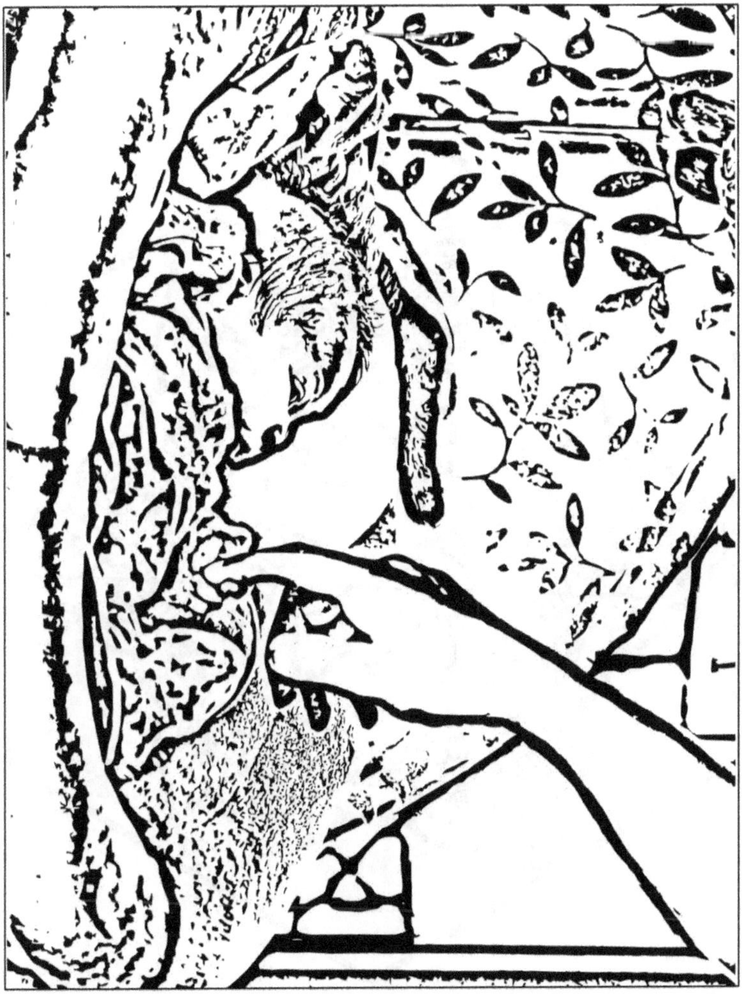

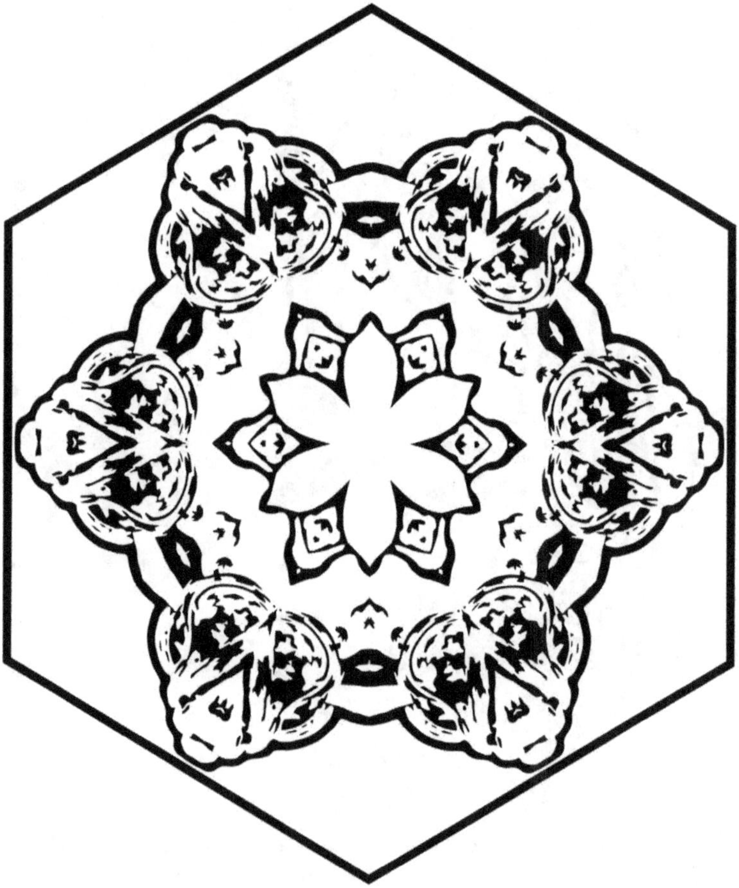

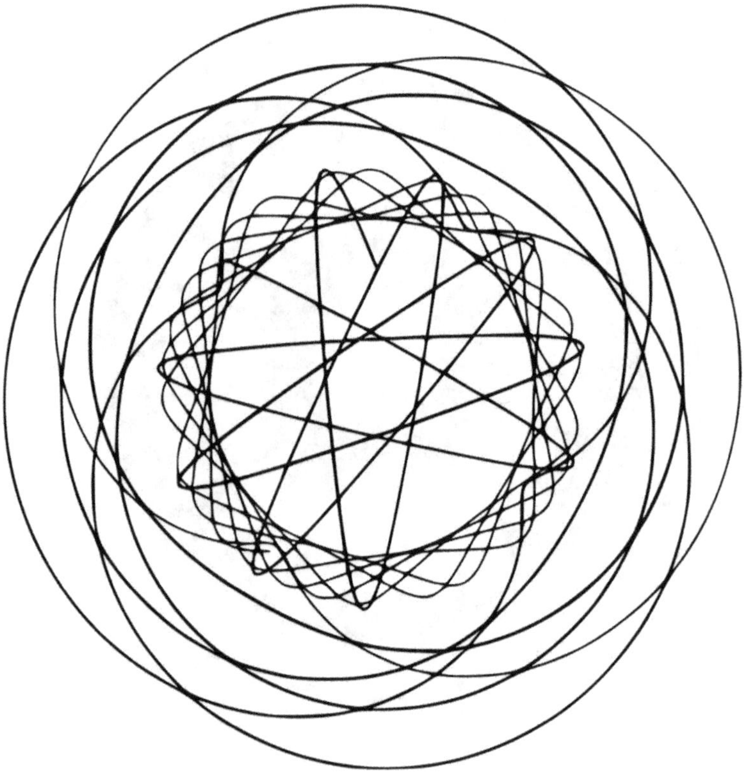

www.ingramcontent.com/pod-product-compliance
Lightning Source LLC
Chambersburg PA
CBHW071644170526
45166CB00003B/1426
* 9 7 8 1 5 1 9 4 5 7 1 6 5 *